26. -

What on Earth? Life in the Wetlands

What on Earth?

A nose like a snorkel!

What uses
its nose like a
snorkel and can
stay underwater
for a long time?

Turn the page for the answer.

Published in 2005 in the United States by Children's Press,
an imprint of Scholastic Library Publishing,
90 Sherman Turnpike, Danbury, CT 06816

ISBN 0-516-25318-2 (Lib. Bdg.)

A CIP catalog record for this title is available from the Library of Congress.

Printed and bound in China.

Editor:	Ronald Coleman
Senior Art Editor:	Carolyn Franklin
DTP Designer:	Mark Williams

Picture Credits: Julian Baker: 8, 9(t), 17; Mark Bergin: 4,
10, 20-21(c), 21(t); Elizabeth Branch: 1, 2, 8(b), 9, 22, 23(t);
Roger Hutchins: 4-5(b), 6-7, 11; Daniel Heuclin, NHPA: 12;
Mirko Stelzner, NHPA: 13; Christopher Ratier, NHPA: 14;
William Paton, NHPA: 15; Hellio and Van Ingen, NHPA: 20;
Martin Wendler, NHPA: 24; Stephen Dalton, NHPA: 25;
Paal Hermansen, NHPA: 26; PhotoDisc: 3, 16, 27, 28, 29;
Digital Vision: 18(b), 23(b); Corbis: 18(r), 19; John Foxx: 31

Cover © Digital Vision

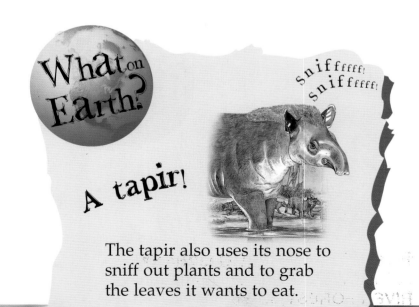

What on Earth?

Sniffffff!
Sniffffff!

A tapir!

The tapir also uses its nose to
sniff out plants and to grab
the leaves it wants to eat.

What on Earth? Life in the Wetlands

CAROLYN SCRACE

children's press

A Division of Scholastic Inc.

NEW YORK • TORONTO • LONDON • AUCKLAND • SYDNEY

MEXICO CITY • NEW DELHI • HONG KONG

DANBURY, CONNECTICUT

Can a terrapin bark?

Go to page 22 for the answer!

Contents

What on Earth?

Clever stickleback!

The male three-spined stickleback builds a nest from bits of underwater plants.

Introduction

Wetlands are not just muddy swamps or murky bogs! They are packed full of amazing plants and animals. Many of these would die without the food, water, and shelter that wetlands provide. Wetlands can be large or small, hot or cold!

Are there different types of wetlands?

Swamps, bogs, fens and marshes are the main types of wetlands. They are found throughout the world. Weather conditions and types of soil make them different from each other.

Are wetlands always wet?

No! Some wetlands are always wet but others dry up during hot times of the year. A wetland only has shallow, slow-moving water. The water is never deep or fast-flowing like in rivers or seas.

What is happening above the water?   Turn the page for the answer!

What Are Wetlands?

Seas and oceans are not wetlands! Large lakes and rivers are not wetlands! A wetland is an area of land that is covered by a shallow body of water for some, or all of the year. Wetlands can be formed if it rains a lot and the water doesn't drain away. Snow that melts and rivers that overflow can also make a wetland.

Knobthorn acacia

Sitatunga

African pygmy goose

African jacana

Look at this picture of an African swamp

This African swamp is a wetland in the middle of a desert. It is the only place where these plants and animals can find water.

Spoonbill

Leopard tortoise

Purple heron

Pirate butterfly

Black-striped rana frog

Pond skater

Anopheles mosquito

African pike

Tiger fish

Jewelled cichlid

African fish eagle

Papyrus

Sitatunga

Hippopotamus

African clawless otter

Malachite kingfisher

Dragonfly

Blister beetle

Nile crocodile

Water lilies

Nile crocodile

Dwarf mouth brooder

Where Are Wetlands?

There are wetlands on every continent in the world except for **chilly** Antarctica. Antarctica is ice-covered. Because the water is frozen there are no wetlands. The Arctic, northern Canada and Russia are nearly as cold as Antarctica but they do have wetland areas.

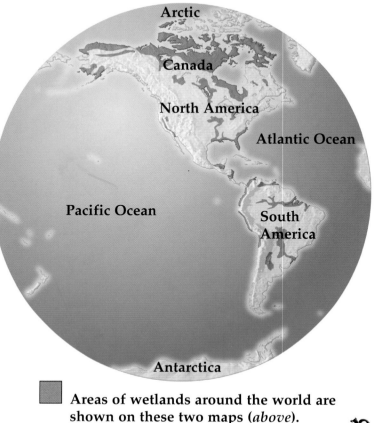

Arctic

Canada

North America

Atlantic Ocean

Pacific Ocean

South America

Antarctica

Areas of wetlands around the world are shown on these two maps (*above*).

where is the world's largest wetland?

The largest wetland is in Brazil, South America. It is enormous — four times the size of the Florida Everglades in North America!

A yellow-dotted toad?

Surinam toad

The Surinam toad is a wetland animal from South America. Those yellow dots on this female's back are eggs. Her babies will hatch on her back and then swim away.

Which continent has the most wetlands?

Arctic

Asia

Russia

Europe

Pacific Ocean

Africa

Indian Ocean

Australia

Antarctica

Africa has more wetlands than any other continent. For a few months each year there is a lot of rain in Africa and the water collects in the wetland areas. During the rest of the year there is little or no rain. Grasses and plants need water to live, so the animals that feed off them move to wetland areas for food.

Do people live in wetlands?

Yes. People all over the world have adapted to living in wetlands.

What on earth is this strange bird?

This weird wetland bird is called the **whale-headed stork** from Africa. It has a massive hooked bill which it uses for finding fish in muddy waters!

Whale-headed stork

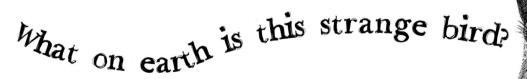

9

What Is A Wetland Food Chain?

When plants die in or around a wetland, their leaves **sink** to the bottom of the water. The dead leaves are eaten by insects that live in the water, and by pond snails and tiny fish. These creatures are then eaten by larger fish, frogs, newts, and birds. This is called a **food chain!**

What are plankton?

Plankton are the smallest plants and animals in the water. They are the beginning of a wetland food chain. Tadpoles and small insects feed on plankton. The dragonfly nymph eats the tadpoles and small insects. The dragonfly nymph then grows into an adult dragonfly that eats other, larger insects. The dragonfly is then eaten by a hungry bird, a spider or even a frog!

Eat and be eaten?

The **great diving beetle** floats to the surface of the water to breathe. It stores air in special tubes in its body. Then it dives down into the water to eat tadpoles, pond snails, and even small fish. Great diving beetles are then eaten by frogs. So what eats a frog? Some snakes, birds and lizards like to eat frogs!

Great diving beetle

Tadpole

10

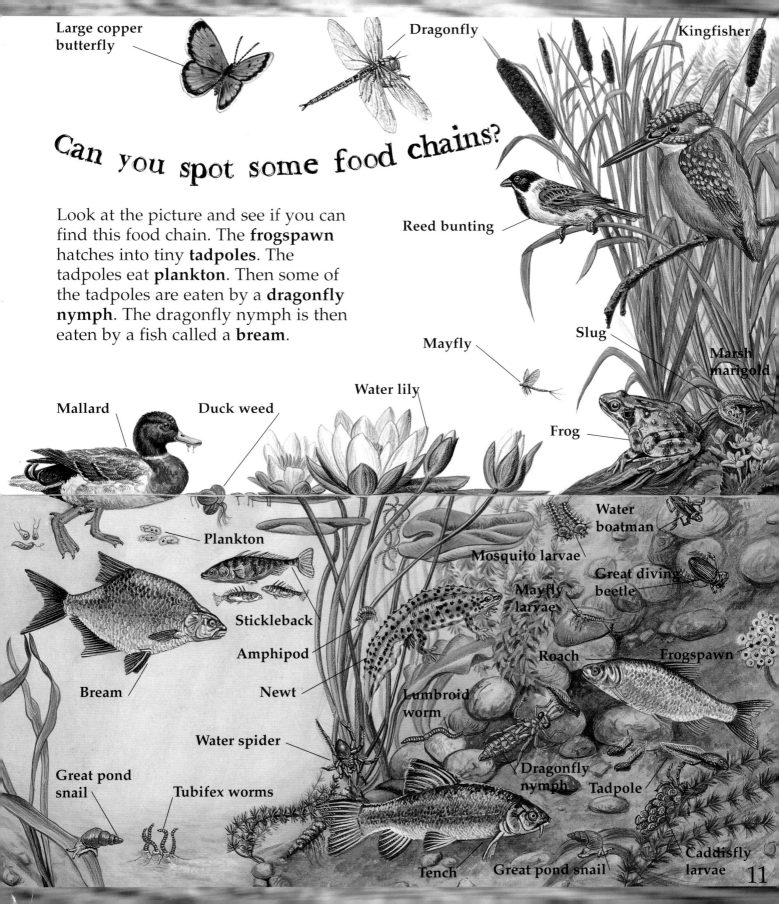

Large copper butterfly

Dragonfly

Kingfisher

Can you spot some food chains?

Look at the picture and see if you can find this food chain. The **frogspawn** hatches into tiny **tadpoles**. The tadpoles eat **plankton**. Then some of the tadpoles are eaten by a **dragonfly nymph**. The dragonfly nymph is then eaten by a fish called a **bream**.

Reed bunting

Slug

Mayfly

Marsh marigold

Water lily

Mallard

Duck weed

Frog

Plankton

Water boatman

Mosquito larvae

Great diving beetle

Mayfly larvae

Stickleback

Roach

Frogspawn

Amphipod

Newt

Bream

Lumbroid worm

Water spider

Dragonfly nymph

Tadpole

Great pond snail

Tubifex worms

Tench

Great pond snail

Caddisfly larvae

11

Are Wetlands All the same?

Swamps, bogs, marshes, and fens are all different types of wetlands. Swamps can be found in fresh water and in salty sea water in hot or cold areas of the world. Swamps usually have trees. Bogs are only found in colder climates and are different from swamps. A thick dark material called **peat** lines the bottom of a bog. Its surface is often completely covered by a green carpet of moss.

Steamy mangrove swamp!

Mangrove trees grow in hot, salt-water swamps. The mangrove trees (below) have special roots that grow out of their trunks and branches. These roots hold the trees firmly in the muddy soil and supply them with food and oxygen.

Almost no oxygen?

Swamp mud contains almost no oxygen. This is why the roots of the mangrove tree grow above the mud — to absorb oxygen.

What Are Marshes and Fens?

Marshes and fens are types of wetlands. Most of the year their soil is either waterlogged or under water. However, they may dry up completely during a very hot summer. Salt marshes are found near the sea. The grasses and plants that grow in these marshes can live in salt-water and can cope with the different levels of sea water caused by tides.

This salt-water marsh (below) is in Africa. An elephant cools down in the muddy water.

What is covered with moss?

A fen. Fens have green and brown moss growing on them. Marshes have none. Also, fens are usually wetter or flooded longer than marshes.

What on Earth?

Do marshes stink?

Yes. Some marshes really do stink. When wetland plants die, they rot, and the process of rotting makes marsh gas that is really stinky!

What plants Are in Wetlands?

Each type of wetland suits a different sort of plant. Plants are very important as they add oxygen to the water. Many of the plants found in wetlands have **adapted** to live in wet conditions. There are three types of plants that live in the wetlands. Some, like reeds, grow out of the water. Others, like water lilies, float on top of the water. Some plants live completely under the water.

What on Earth?

As big as a water lily!

The largest water lily grows in the Amazon River basin in South America. It can be the size of a big round kitchen table!

Can plants eat insects?

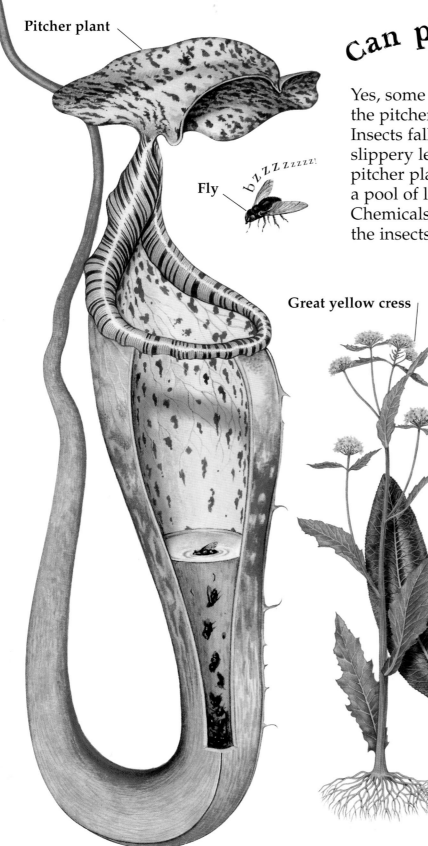

Pitcher plant

Fly

bzzz zzzzzz!

Yes, some plants, such as the pitcher plant, can. Insects fall down the slippery leaves of the pitcher plant to land in a pool of liquid inside. Chemicals then digest the insects.

Some wetland plants are poisonous. Others can be used as medicines. Butterbur can cure headaches, fever and colds. Horseradish can calm a toothache. Don't touch celery-leaved crowfoot as it will make your skin blister!

Horseradish

Great yellow cress

Celery-leaved crowfoot

Butterbur

What Birds and Animals Live There?

Many birds and animals live in or near a wetland. Some of them have special feet to stop them from **sinking** into the wet mud. Both the sitatunga (see page 7) and caribou have toes that spread apart as they walk on swampy wetland. The jacana (see page 6), has feet with long thin toes that help it to walk on floating leaves!

The godwit is a wading bird. Wading birds have long legs and beaks which they use for catching food.

What sweats pink goo?

A hippopotamus has pink sweat that keeps it cool! It is the largest animal that lives in swamps. It weighs as much as four cars and can open its mouth wide enough to eat a table. And it has tusks as long as a baseball bat!

Why the long neck?

Herons are another type of wading bird. They wade into shallow water on their long legs. Using their long necks and beaks they reach down into the water to find small crabs and shellfish.

What on Earth?

What makes an amazing journey?

What migrates all the way from chilly wetlands in the Arctic to hot, steamy wetlands in South America?

Small birds like sandpipers and plovers! These tiny birds make this incredible journey in search of food and warmth.

Are There Any Fish?

Fish that live in swampy areas usually have thin bodies to help them to swim easily through the dense vegetation. Most of these fish can live in water where there is little oxygen. Some, like the lung fish, can even breathe air. A fish called the mailed catfish uses its stomach to breathe!

Pike

Can fish walk?

Yes, mudskippers (below) can skip across mud on their fins faster than you can walk. They can even climb up tree roots! Mudskippers breathe partly through their skin.

Fierce fish?

Pike (above) are fierce fish that are often found in reed swamps. They use their strong jaws to catch their prey which includes ducklings and coots. The pike will stay hidden among the plants until its prey passes and then it darts out and grabs it.

Mudskipper

Painful pincers?

Crayfish are not fish. They are crustaceans, related to lobsters and crabs. Crayfish live in lakes, rivers and swamps. They have two large pincers or claws which they use to catch their prey. Crayfish hunt at night, and eat snails, small fish, and other water animals.

Crayfish

What on Earth?

40-year-old fish?

Yes. Some carp can live for up to 40years! Carp live in lakes and slow moving rivers. They use four feelers in the corners of their mouth to find food in the muddy water.

Do Scary Creatures Live There?

Crocodiles and alligators live in tropical swamps. Many snakes and turtles live in wetlands, and some of them have special ways of catching food. The mata-mata turtle from South America has ragged skin around its neck which looks like pieces of food. Small fish looking for a meal get too close and are sucked into the turtle's mouth.

All insects living in swamps are able to breathe air. Some push tubes, like snorkels, out of the water to breathe through.

Woof woof?

Terrapins bark when angry! The painted terrapin lives in ponds, lakes, and marshes in North and South America.

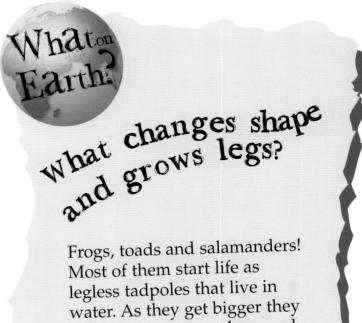

What on Earth?

What changes shape and grows legs?

Frogs, toads and salamanders! Most of them start life as legless tadpoles that live in water. As they get bigger they change shape, grow legs, and then live on land!

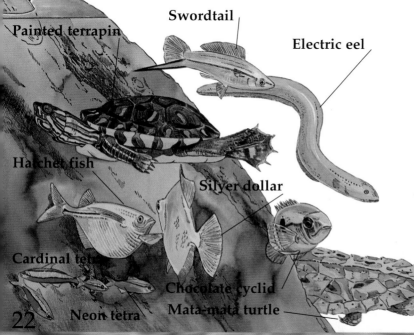

Painted terrapin

Swordtail

Electric eel

Hatchet fish

Silver dollar

Cardinal tetra

Chocolate cyclid

Neon tetra

Mata-mata turtle

What is the World's biggest snake?

The anaconda! A fully grown anaconda can be as long as three cars. It squeezes its prey to death and can take over a week to digest a large animal!

Dragonfly

Anaconda

Caiman

Crocodile or alligator?

Crocodiles and alligators look very similar. To tell the difference look at their teeth. A crocodile's lower front teeth can be seen when it closes its mouth but an alligator's teeth are hidden!

Why Are Wetlands So Important?

Wetlands help to save the world's coastlines. The roots of wetland plants hold soil in place which stops it from being swept away by strong ocean waves and currents. Wetlands can prevent flooding. They act like giant sponges, soaking up water and slowing it down. They also filter the water that passes through them, making it cleaner.

Wetlands are very important because the survival of many endangered species relies on the water, food, and shelter they find there.

The Brazilian tapir is an endangered wetland animal.

What on Earth?

Can wetlands keep the planet clean?

Yes. Wetlands trap many chemicals that pollute our planet. Chemicals such as fertilizers, mercury and lead, and bacteria that cause diseases, can all be filtered out of water that passes through a wetland.

Are Wetlands In Danger?

In the last 100 years, over half of the world's wetlands have disappeared. People have drained them to build roads and cities or turned them into farmland. They have built canals and dams that take water away from wetland areas to supply it to cities and factories. Wetlands have been **destroyed** by mining and by logging. Some wetlands have been poisoned when harmful chemicals from factories and farming were poured into them. Many countries now protect their wetland areas.

How would you survive in a wetland?

There is plenty of food to be found in a wetland, such as edible berries and plants, fish, and shellfish. But be careful because there is an animal or two that would like to eat you instead!

Wetland dangers

Hippopotamus The best way to stay safe is never to get between a hippopotamus and water!

Alligator Keep well away from an alligator. Don't throw anything at it and never try to feed one!

Anaconda Stay well away from the water. An anaconda is slow to move on land but sure to catch you underwater!

What to take checklist

Wear long trousers tucked into knee-high rain boots to keep your legs dry. Carry a stick to test the ground for sogginess. You don't want to sink in the mud!

Take a fishing rod to catch your dinner and a box of matches to light a fire to cook the fish. You will need a map to find your way and a two-way radio in case you need help! Cover yourself in bug spray to keep the insects from biting you. Do not drink the water — bring your own!

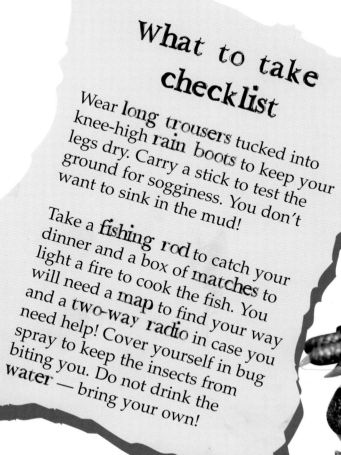

Wetland Facts

In the last one hundred years, humans have destroyed half of the world's wetlands!

Nearly two thirds of all fish caught throughout the world are hatched in mangrove swamps!

Pantanal is a huge wetland in South America. Endangered species like jaguars, ocelots, giant anteaters and giant armadillos and marsh deer live here.

World Wetlands' Day is held each year on February 2nd. It gives leaders from different countries a chance to talk about wetlands.

Moss growing on top of some bogs can hold up to ten times its weight in water.

A hippopotamus can hold its breath under water for up to ten minutes.

Humans have changed the nature of three fifths of the world's largest rivers. By altering the flow of these rivers, many wetlands have been lost.

Pelican

Glossary

adapted the way a plant or animal has changed to survive in its habitat

continent one of seven very large land masses in the world

chemicals substances used in a chemical process

digest to break down food so it can be absorbed

endangered species plants or animals in danger of disappearing forever, (usually because of changes that have taken place in their habitats)

fertilizer substance added to soil to make it more fertile

food chain natural sequence of predator and prey

migrates/migration the movement of birds or animals often across vast distances, usually in spring or autumn

nymph a young insect

oxygen the gas that all living things need to breath

pollute to make air, water or soil dirty or harmful to plants and animals that live there

Frog

What Do You Know About Wetlands?

1. Are wetlands ever deep?

2. Which continent has the most wetlands?

3. What eats a great diving beetle?

4. Why do the roots of the mangrove tree grow above the mud?

5. What happens if you touch celery-leaved crowfoot?

6. Which fish can live for up to 40 years?

7. How can you tell the difference between a crocodile and an alligator?

8. Can a terrapin bark?

9. How long does an anaconda take to digest a large animal?

10. Do wetlands keep the planet clean?

Go to page 32 for the answers!

Can you guess how fast a hippopotamus can swim under water?

Index

Pictures are shown in **bold** type.

Answers

1. No (See page 5)
2. Africa (See page 9)
3. The frog (See page 10)
4. To absorb oxygen (See page 13)
5. It will make your skin blister! (See page 17)
6. Carp (See page 21)
7. Look at their teeth (See page 23)
8. Yes — if it's angry! (See page 22)
9. Over a week (See page 23)
10. Yes (See page 25)

An adult hippopotamus can swim underwater at a speed of 4.9 miles (8 kilometers) per hour. That is a fast walking pace for a human.